Bismillah Hir Rahman Nir Raheem

(In the name of Allah the Beneficent, the Merciful)

Contents

The Owl

From a restive place, calmly watching and observing. Thinking quietly to itself. Gets quite annoyed at the smallest of creatures. Shows anger usually because of it's own behaviour. Talks at a time when everyone is trying to sleep and his talk can put you too sleep. They say he's wise they say he's stupid. If it's one thing certain about the owl he usually looks down at you. A silent hunter that loves the night and also prefers a time of solitude, when he can find when it which is never too soon. Is at times troublesome and weary. The owl likes a good talk usually by himself. He may get a response but not the one he was looking for. The owls favourite time is his sleep hardly seen but usually heard. They make other creatures of flight afraid. At times it seems to be wise and other times its timing can be off. It's uniquely distinctly identifiable in appearance and sound. They are known to be very active at night only. They blend in well with their surroundings which makes it hard to spot them unless you are avidly searching for them in a given environment. They are almost always found living alone. They also have great vision and sense of smell. They can fly very quickly even though most of the time you see one it may be perched and not moving at all. Owls have a routine that starts their day and it is interesting to see. They are very meticulous when it comes to their appearance. They will spend their first few hours awake preening and stretching. They use their tools to clean themselves and then make sure their tools are clean. It doesn't leave its roost without this activity taking place unless they are scared off by predators. They are extremely good at stalking their prey, patiently waiting for the right time to swoop down and get them.

The Shark

A proper predator that is wild and powerful. There's nothing like a good drop to set him off. With cold dark empty eyes it's as ruthless as its bite. It sees its prey but cannot see its own weak spot. Easily fed and also soothed by a gentle touch. It is guaranteed to bite with an excellent sense of smell. Rushes to its food and spends most of its time with a few extra smiles. It's quite happy being the scariest fish around however a playful time leaves it spooked. If there is one thing sure about the shark is that he doesn't like you with a passion that only fits a top guy. It has a keen notion of being the apex predator and loves his work. It is inspired to set fear in others. The sharks favourite time is during the hunt. The shark never stops moving, it loves to travel long distances to get its favourite meal, and find its favourite partner. A trip worthy of making since the shark cant stop moving it prefers to go far places where new types of food can be found. It as a top predator loves to keep the regulation of other species. Sometimes turning on its own. When a shark is hungry its best to not be around. The best place for a shark is in the midst of all the others, so that others know that the shark is the one that will cause the funk to be instilled in everyone else. Whose got the funk the sharks got the funk.

The lizard

It doesn't know when it's in someone else's home. It thinks it owns the place. Usually runs into trouble and causes problems for the sensible folk. The lizard speaks a foul language and behaves in a most inappropriate manner. It makes everyone feel uneasy especially the ladies. The best answer to the lizard is the boot. Can be quite smart and usually likes to make an interesting display of its behaviour. However it doesn't like to make you feel at home. If it's one thing sure about the lizard is that spending time with it will lead you astray because they don't know the path that should be walked on. They spend most of their time stuck to something else. Usually ready to leave you with a problem. Interesting and diverse, the lizard features itself in many forms and many places. If it loses its smile it can grow another one. Most of them are silent and only prefer body language, rare amongst them are those that create verbal sounds. They like a different set of clothing in contrast to their places according to the mood they are in. A fantastic sense of smell that tastes really good to them determining what it is that the air around them is like. You wont find them near the big freeze, anywhere but there. A very grippy individual they love to climb in the most unusual of places.

The Monkey

A most unusual of creatures, awkward and pretty clever but not so pretty. He's usually stuck in a world of mocking and laughter and also deception. Not happy with his comrades. Ingenious problem solver, likes a laugh usually at your expense. Has a good time most of the time. Feeling quite pleased with himself. Loves to have fun with his woman but has to be careful a monkey doesn't know his own woman sometimes. Gets into trouble and makes a lot of trouble. Dangerous and usually ends up in a fight. Caring only a few times. The monkey loves his food and food is his life. Searching all day and thinking only of his next meal. and likes laziness even when its time to party. A monkey at a party wants to be the centre of attention and the star of the show. Loud boisterous and rarely quite naughty. Monkey madness monkey business, tricky and loves a laugh. Good at making building only to usually ruin it for himself and others. If you want fun a monkey is your man. Monkey's and trees a place of most enjoyable activity and also a place of safety. They cannot live without the tree. Vocalisation and body movements with the most odd facial expressions to communicate. Affection and peace amongst each other is created by looking and grooming each other. They mate for life and become distressed when separated. Playing and tricks and games on each other and also causing trouble for the other. Asserting dominance upon a rival with any means necessary. The monkey is truly a mad creature.

The Bee

The most loved and loved to work, inspired by the Almighty to collect the best and only that which is beneficial. Careful and gentle, moves with utmost agility a wing woosh. And a make of a most beautiful sweet drink, a nectar that helps everyone. Bee plays a most beautiful game, one that benefits all those who encounter it. A flower, a person an insect an exchange of good words. However they can annoy and be quite enjoyable in their company. Bees love each other and smell great. Saves itself and those with it and if need be takes out its enemy only to lose its life. Although prefers to work, it loves a good flight. Flying at a speed the cruise control function would be envious of. The only bug that makes food that people can eat. Its food improves your mental ability. Makes you smarter and sweeter. Many other life forms are dependant on this creature that is so good to all of them. Taking only the best and leaving just what you need. If its one thing good said about anything or anyone it's the bees knees. A keen sense of smell, their home is uniquely fragrant. If its one thing the bees love its work and its work to the end. Unique facial recognition ability, they like to tell those apart. The disappearance of this most useful creature will leave a vacuum in your life. Most loved and most used the bee loves and loves to bee.

The Ant

The hard working soldier, worker everyday a day of preparation, scurrying along busy in its duty. inspired by the One to make a better civilization. in search of provision and making a better life. Life is work and work is good. Day in day out it works in praise to the Almighty for giving it strength 100 times its own self. Hard compact tough and energetic, constantly moving. Building energy and moving at a measured distribution. The Qadr of Allah. Its path it makes it finds it travels, it's the constant traveller. The ant is a beautiful maumin. In search of a sweet nectar, it is friendly with its own troops. moving steadily through the pattern of the path set forth by its inspiration. Walk is life and life is respectful, and ready all the time battling on. The path that it follows will one day end, its reward is its life, a good existence in service to the One. Ant like in behaviour. They talk quite well living amongst giants and wild birds and creatures. When it rains the ants are already sheltered sensing a down pour, nestling away waiting for the storm to subside. Before its back to the days work. Everyday is a great day in the life of an Ant. An ant is best when its busy.

The Rat

The rat ever ready to squirm its way amongst you. Causes problems and runs away. Skittish, unworthy and not reliable. Spreads chaos and ill health. Unkempt unclean and greedy in nature. Never a good word or a feeling from them. Lurks in the darkness as the presence of light makes it afraid. Doesn't l'ke to share, would give up to save its own skin, its own friends. Cowardly in nature only seen when drawn out by fire or hunger. Untrustworthy spreads mischief and lies, ignoble and vile. Rat is only good amongst its own people. Even then its a rat salad.

Social and affectionate they enjoy the company of others just like themselves. Without a friend they become lonely and depressed. They often succumb to peer pressure and copy others in their behaviour. They can last quite long without water. Verbally express themselves with laughter when happy. Cleaner only on the outside when in a quiet place. Excellent at overcoming obstacles with an acute sense of balance. They love a good snack. They make a nice trip when its involving travelling large distances. And love swimming cause their good at it. Their smart and can learn quite fast. And loved to be taught tricks. Have an excellent knack for napping. The personality of a rat is larger than life. And they love to form bonds with others.

The Snake

A striking predator quick and graceful, cold, dark and mysterious. Guaranteed to bring harm in to your life weaves its way through. The place to leave it is on its own far from your own home. Very keen hunter has a very lazy attitude particularly after a meal. Found hidden amongst the surroundings, enjoys its movement particularly past the river. Doesn't like water unless of course it lives their. Snake warns or sometimes its too late, charmed easily by a praise or two a melodious voice leaves it waiting to be placed somewhere else. The best way to deal with a snake is to send it far from yourself its weakest point being the top of its head. If their is one thing sure about the snake its not a good friend but loves itself to be by itself. Solitairy at heart. They respond more to movement rather than to sound.

The charmer just happens to play a song for you and not for the snake. A deception. More dangerous are the ones in the water. Water and this creature turn into a deadly machine. When it comes to their diet they are very flexible. They don't blink but give you the death stare. They don't like the cold and if it's cold you won't find them there. Very sensitive to movements, vibrations and change in light. Don't often require a meal as they prefer an empty stomach. Strictly meat eaters.

They don't like milk poured on them.

The Fox

The first word that comes to mind is that its witty and quite agile and quick. Clever at problem solving. Causing problems and also quick to run from them. Finds a way past its predators. When its hungry its best to stay away from it. It never sees what belongs to itself, everything is up for grabs. Notoriously dangerous at observational skills. Astute and quite skillfull. Heartwarming and a keen sense of whats going to go down. And the first to take itself with its comrades away from danger. Loves to run out amongst the open sky. Can send itself quite happily to where it needs to be. Harmful to the young. The fox is better off outside. The fox will tell you what you need to do. The fox's curl is a serene moment.

Whether its cosy hollow, a den or a burrow underground or the earth the fox is right at home. When it comes to looking after the young ones the fox provides very well. The elder provides valuable experience lessons for the young. Springs on their feet they like to pounce right on top of their prey. Incredibly adaptable with a fondness for night time wanderings. Very good at settling in your home when your least expecting it. Envied for its luxurious coat.

The Tiger

Elusive you only see it close to death. A hunter preys on its victim with stealth and surrounding camouflage. Mysterious, wild and ferocious, does not like confined places. Prefers solitude to social interaction and enjoys its hunt. Meal time is a place of contentment. Not wise to stare it in the face. Running to it is admirable, weakness lies on top of its head. One giant ladel bang.

Lazy during the day they prefer the sharpness of the morning or the invisibility of the night. They hiss and huff before an attack and roar only to communicate with others. They allow the females and young ones to eat first, rarely arguing or fighting and prefer to simply wait their turn. The status of the tiger by its marking and behaviour suggest that it is a most noble regal creature.

The Dog

A companion to your bad time. Follows orders even it doesn't know what it means, eager, friendly and reliable because you know that a dog will be a dog. Looked down upon society feelings of pity towards it from all sides, It doesn't really think it just acts. Does what it says on the tin. Kept tied gets frustrated, it doesn't discriminate happy to join someone who can tell it what to do. Makes a mess of its space. unclean and doesn't look after itself. Will reduce your benefit and waste your deeds and time. Prefers to be in a low place. Not wise to keep dogs unless their on guard duty or out for hunting. Only the fool and the dog get along well together.

Can understand only few words and those that are familiar to its liking. Intelligent enough to know which way leads to the food. Can be very useful in saving the lives of others. Can only hear what others like it can hear. Love to travel and can wrack up the air miles. Very good at comforting a distressed soul. Ready to uplift your mood. When treated the right way and got ready they know its time for work. Very good listeners. With the right behaviour they become loved by all. They are constantly in contact with the ground unless over excited.

The Bear

Nurturing friendly only to its own. Has a sweet tooth. Ferocious and confident quite brazen. particularly slow unless he doesn't like you. A great heart and compassionate. A noble being unless of course it gets hungry or annoyed. With powerful strength its best not to be around them. Wise and experienced a bear knows its path well. Loves children and young ones and enjoys life. Lives a tiring time and its resources are limited. Finds what it loves and knows what it sees.

Curious to see who is over there and have Technicolor vision. The best sense of smell particularly before its feeding time. Too many bears leads to laziness, With a bite power that will leaves your pins rolling. Has to eat as much as it needs too and needs a lot. Bear power in the water is exceptional, a large distance traversed in a continuous stride. Bowlegged with better balance and quite active at night.

The Crow

Noisy and selfish, attracts to much attention and seeks to annoy. It may get its morsel, however it transgresses its limits, and knows only the problems that it itself creates and is familiar with. Its intuitiveness is based on behavior it studies. Most of the time the behavior it causes itself. In groups amongst themselves, or as a pair, the individual they cause an uproar. The crow behavior is usually of a mocking nature, laughter. Positive attributes as found in birds such as defending territory boundaries, protecting their mate, or defending some other resource. Crows do have one endearing characteristic that is apparently not shared by other birds. They will get to know people as individuals.

The Earthworm

Strong and mighty the earthworm burrows through the dirt as if its moving life a fish through water. Consuming what its with and its nourishment. Inspired towards heavy movement and reaching far out ahead. However water brings out the worm from the earth. The rain worm, the night crawler and the angleworm. Strongworm can move about and eat the same time. Potassium and nitrogen, two favourite nutrients.

The Spider

The spider ever busy making homes a property investor, however its home is the weakest you will find, guaranteed to bring you provision by capturing a mobile flying object. The female is the scariest even the male knows it's doomed against her. Hunger that it finds itself making a creative pattern designed and inspired also to protect and provide supervision. The spider at most times is finding itself useless until its prey steps into its trap. Happy to make itself a nice place that even the female might admire so much so that dinner is served with the host as the main course. A solitairy creature most of the time happy to be amongst himself and waiting for its next meal to arrive.

Spiders chose prey smaller than itself. Spiders' primary niche in nearly every system is controlling populations. Some families, do this through passive hunting with their signature webs. Others, like do this through active hunting. Spiders turn on spiders and other similar to it and a great source of food for other hunters. Though many dislike them they end up infesting your home. Weaving a thread a fine fabric so durable its practically steel. Steel jacket technique is not difficult for a spider.

The Goat

Friendly and approachable, however it is quite stubborn by itself and becomes more agreeable when it finds a familiar looking species. Happy to eat most of what it finds and what it finds is mostly green. The goat has a balance that others envy and a sturdy kick with its walk, upright and firm on its hooves. The goat moves quickly happily with its friends and its familiar company. Hardy and resilient however it knows not its limits when it comes to its promiscuous behavior.

A difficult individual doesn't like to listen or do what it needs to be told. It particularly thinks that it's not really a goat but a most agile athlete designed for the mountain edge. Balanced precariously quite easily and comfortably smirking at its hunter. Who just waits out the prey. If its one thing that is certain about the goat it tastes like a fine dish on a summer afternoon. Strings of meat and you have to be careful, the goat likes to think he's king.

The Ox

Strong and sturdy heavy set and stubborn, a powerful creature with wealth milk and meat. However the ox although it loves to hit it knows no finesse or gentleness other than to its own who it usually ends up harming. Used for many as means to an end a heavy burden that it carries only to make it further a far into its inspired behavior. Useful in giving it lots of work to do to make it better. Keep it preoccupied as it is known to cause trouble for all others.

Sleep little and can laboriously toil with their trouble. They work for many times and our more steady than most others. The symbol of fortitude and strength, and a lack of intelligence. With old age, misfortune and adversity but good at providing shelter in harsh conditions.

The Cat

Territorial and very independent. Useful in looking after themselves. Sleek , flexible, and agile. The cat captures its prey with careful quiet steps, stalking its prey and waits for the opportune moment and pounces on it. Tunnel like vision but that's expected as its eyes are on the front of its face. It tends not to see what is above. Very intelligent and makes itself known to its environment. Walks and talks like a chairman. Appreciative of its provision and clean behaviour and walks amongst us like it is one of us. A very beneficial sleep and resourceful creature. Provides very well and hunts like a champ.

They don't know how to reverse very well from going down a tree. Coveted for their worth and what they can provide to others, treasured and kept in a place in their own comfortable environment. Exceptional at sending itself above many times its own self. Can leap for joy or for fright.

A unique style of itself above its smile. And enjoy temperatures varying with the water. Swift at movement and a playful manner, loves its games that make it feel uplifted.

The Albatross

Quite calm most of the time, a stretched wingspan folded well, on the rocks where the water is nearby. Inspired to live near the ocean drift, the sea breeze is its best friend, gliding along the great expanse. A wild cry and a run on the shore with a take off that is impeccable. The albatross soars for days on end. The master of the air current. It glides in a smooth observant manner. Quietly watching from a far a place of freedom, held upright by the Almighty and kept calm with its water reflection shimmering in response to its quite movement. A shadow moving along the surface of the water. The albatross is the best at what it does a masterful longhaul flight. In a world envious by all those who see it. Its arms reaching to the east and west to the tip of the edge of the world. it however flies south when it needs to. The migration on the current drifting again like the 1st class flight. The inspired peaceful bird of the current. Its wing built for a far observant flight. Fish is on the menu.

The Donkey

Ready to move with you, only good at bearing your burden. Pleasant unless he kicks like a mule or opens his mouth. A useful baggage handler. Doesn't understand other than where its food is. Keeps asking for more baggage quite good at doing nothing. Is a brute with little sense. Doesn't know itself or anyone else properly, and senses danger too late. Is quite amused at its own sense. Since very little happens between the ears. Likes to travel on a long journey, travelling companion guaranteed to provide a generous seat. Flight animals that survive by running away. Donkey knows its territory but doesnt know who its supposed to be guarding and who too chase away. the search for food kept them mentally stimulated in the environment. A donkey learns according too its behaviour and related to hunger and its use in movement.

The donkey will never get involved in an activity if it considers it to be unsafe. With proper maintenance and care, they can live for many years. Love company and those that are on their four feet like them. Their large ears make them have a very acute sense of hearing. And helps to keep them cool. Independent thinking and decision making usually a poor choice. Curious by nature and the rain is no good for them. They do like to learn although it takes a long time. Love a good roll on the ground and they enjoy their life in that way the most.

The Elephant

Heavy set and a good friend patient calm with a sweet tooth. A good recognition of itself and its family. Strong and intelligent, the ant is a frightening creature to the most gentle of beings. Reliable is the elephant ready to traverse the distance with its family. A better way forward. Furious at his enemies, a sound ready to blare. it loves its self and loves to be loved. It has a very careful manner, protective and joyful. The elephant loves its life with its family and friends. A good company to share some sticks of nourishment. At home in the water playful and needy. Loves to play and enjoy its life, strength of character a proper maumin.

The Leaf Bug

Looks like any other bow. The place it feels best is when it can't be seen. It wants to look like all the rest. Alone and reclusive prefers very little to very much more. Use of very little resources. Quite adept at being a leaf. Except this leaf doesn't float down it crawls its way past the other leaves. Likes a display makes a picture look like a scene. Prefers not to be looked at and rather be left alone unless its time to display. Doesn't fight but maneuvers itself out of the picture. Cold weakness left inside a firm outer shell. Prefers some old path, place and root. Although it fits in with any structure even if it's quite odd, it doesn't like being told where to go.

Here are two extracts from my next book.

The Stones are Speaking:

The Sun

Fusion mostly and Fission sparingly, efficient, a blaze , a storm and flares. A containment. A Source of well being and a difficult state. A Turbulent and destructive force necessary for existence. It is spherical and pulsating. Impossible to look into without any instrumentation or else you'll left in the dark. It is continuous and cosmic, consistent and generous. It's been damned by the people who shirked it. Made to be placed in the fire from blaze to blaze. It allows us to move about in this world. A very specific mass and mostly of that which is the entire system. Many think that the sun will consume the earth, but before that it will rendered asunder and brought back closer to the disc, a very warm day. Four into one makes one heavy particle. Travelling on its own path reached a speed that even man has beaten. Differential rotation all at once and with a few spots darkened due to different temperatures. Generates a solar wind that travels faster than it self.

Perfectly spherical the disc world contains a gravitational force that won't let it fall apart. The core keeps multiplying fusion four by one, as a result the energy released allows it to disperse as it is continuously trying to create more mass, its not happy that it is not completely 100% of the system. But its own size tells itself you can't go anywhere other than your existing mass and circuit through the milky way. Movement never stops it and it never transgresses its limits. It send out parts of itself to keep the mass at the space occupied. It can't take up all the room and its loves itself. It seeks permission every day and every day it keeps rising from the same place as it always has. One of these days it will turn on itself and be sent back the way it came. Exothermic pressure sent in each direction and a gravitational force completely balanced in its self contained equilibrium.

A random walk taken to the surface, its like zig zags to the front line.

The sun stone is totally one.

The Moon

Soft white light, luminous and a most beautiful companion. many phases and attraction. Gives us the time to tell our months. Reflective in appearance and a mood that changes. Temperamental and barren. Without light it is only a rock. Creates a force that has an effect on the elements. Appearance changes with time returns to itself and produces night light for the brief place between spaces. Damned for the fire as it misled people with its way. A false and deceptive appearance leaves only to return with a change of state. Inconsistent in appearance and a balance guaranteed to fulfill its task. Does not transgress its path. Made with a piece of the earth cosmic and tied to the earth and not allowed to leave its path unless given permission. The moon is only here half the time.

Cosmic neighbor stays where it is most of the time on its way. It shows the same face most of the time. War weary and quite bruised. Craters on the surface and mountains, boulders and moon dust. A different time zone on the moon in its own zone. A shift of its place and movement in relation to any other moment.

The place where time moves at a different pace. Moving through spaces and places and stopping on itself and others.

This big rock has a surface seen just for the briefest of moments. And it's particularly obstinate in its behavior.

Its quite often that I find writing amoosing as I have the necessary koalafications. Please provide a copy to your owl fella, Im not squidding with you. He'll have a whale of a time.

Jazāk Allāhu Khayran

(May Allah reward you with goodness)

www.ingramcontent.com/pod-product-compliance
Lightning Source LLC
Chambersburg PA
CBHW071331310526
45789CB00017B/2258